The Wonderful Story of Christmas

CLAUDE LAFORTUNE

NOVALIS

To my seven grandchildren, whom I adore:
Guillaume, Dominique, Catherine, Raphaëlle,
Nicolas, Margot and François.

Anne

Joachim

Mary is born

I am going to tell you a story. It is a story you may already know, but it is such a good one that people never get tired of hearing or reading it. I will tell it in my own way, using my imagination just a little bit. Here is the wonderful story of Christmas.

Let's travel 2000 years back in time to a small house in Nazareth, which is in Galilee. (You can find Nazareth on a map. It is a city in Israel.) This is the home of Anne and Joachim. Right now, Anne and Joachim are probably the happiest people in the world. Why are they so happy? Well, believe it or not, even though Anne is an old woman, she has just given birth to her first child. They name their beautiful baby girl "Mary."

Mary as a baby

Did you know that, in one ancient language, Mary meant "filled with light"? In another language, her name meant "princess of the sea." What a lovely name!

Just like other children, our little princess learns to walk and to say her first words. With each passing day, she grows taller and more beautiful. She is kind and willing to help others. But she is also quite capable of mischief and loves to tease her friends.

Mary as a little girl

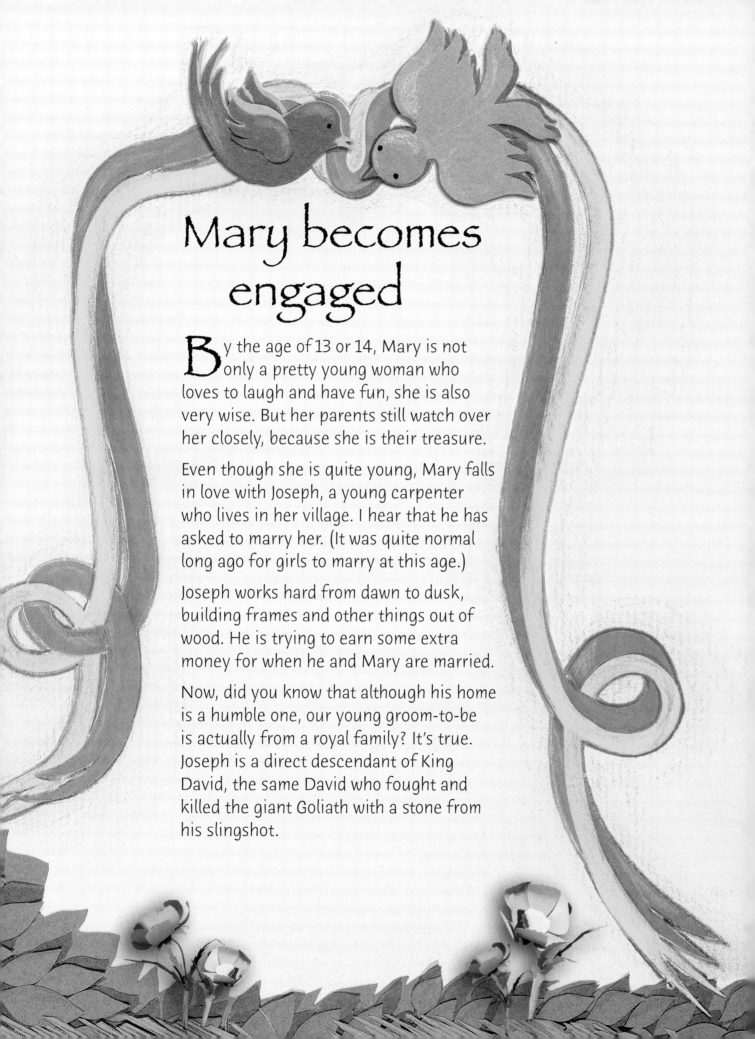

Mary becomes engaged

By the age of 13 or 14, Mary is not only a pretty young woman who loves to laugh and have fun, she is also very wise. But her parents still watch over her closely, because she is their treasure.

Even though she is quite young, Mary falls in love with Joseph, a young carpenter who lives in her village. I hear that he has asked to marry her. (It was quite normal long ago for girls to marry at this age.)

Joseph works hard from dawn to dusk, building frames and other things out of wood. He is trying to earn some extra money for when he and Mary are married.

Now, did you know that although his home is a humble one, our young groom-to-be is actually from a royal family? It's true. Joseph is a direct descendant of King David, the same David who fought and killed the giant Goliath with a stone from his slingshot.

An angel visits Mary

One morning, shortly before the wedding, Anne and Joachim are out buying food and other things for the celebration. Mary is at home by herself, spinning wool.

Suddenly, the room is filled with a blinding light!

"Greetings, O Princess of the sea, of the heavens and of the earth," says a voice that seems to come from another world.

"Who are you?" she whispers.

"Do not be afraid, Mary," the voice says. "I am the Angel Gabriel. I have come to tell you that God has chosen you from among all women. You are to have a child who will bring peace, love and light on earth. You will name the child 'Jesus.' He will be the Son of God."

"Is this possible? I, Mary of Nazareth, am going to give birth to God's Son?" she asks. She is dazed by the angel's words.

"Yes, Mary," the angel says. "You will be the mother of God."

Then the light and the voice are gone.

Mary can hardly believe what is going to happen to her. Filled with joy, she sings what she feels deep down in her heart:

"As a bird flies up into the heavens, I let my gratitude soar
to the One who has done great things for me!"

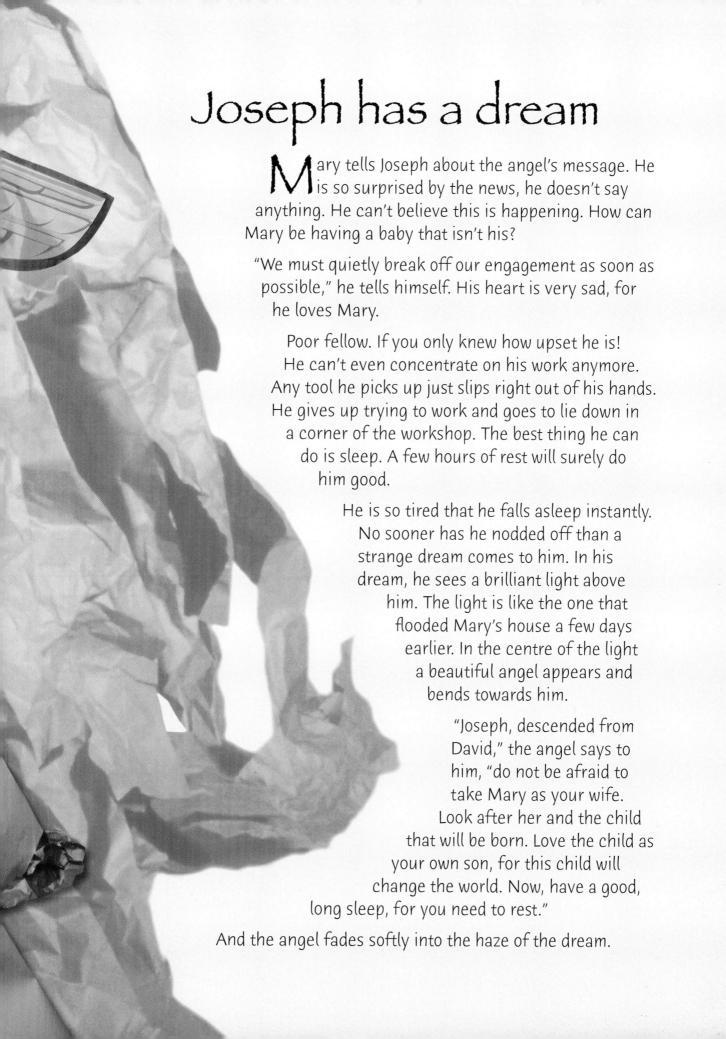

Joseph has a dream

Mary tells Joseph about the angel's message. He is so surprised by the news, he doesn't say anything. He can't believe this is happening. How can Mary be having a baby that isn't his?

"We must quietly break off our engagement as soon as possible," he tells himself. His heart is very sad, for he loves Mary.

Poor fellow. If you only knew how upset he is! He can't even concentrate on his work anymore. Any tool he picks up just slips right out of his hands. He gives up trying to work and goes to lie down in a corner of the workshop. The best thing he can do is sleep. A few hours of rest will surely do him good.

He is so tired that he falls asleep instantly. No sooner has he nodded off than a strange dream comes to him. In his dream, he sees a brilliant light above him. The light is like the one that flooded Mary's house a few days earlier. In the centre of the light a beautiful angel appears and bends towards him.

"Joseph, descended from David," the angel says to him, "do not be afraid to take Mary as your wife. Look after her and the child that will be born. Love the child as your own son, for this child will change the world. Now, have a good, long sleep, for you need to rest."

And the angel fades softly into the haze of the dream.

Mary and Joseph get married

The moment he wakes up, Joseph feels once again the peace he thought he had lost.

"Mary is the woman I love and want to marry," he cries out. His heart is bubbling over with joy.

It is the evening of one of the loveliest spring days ever. Joseph, along with his family and a few friends, makes his way towards Mary's house. Following the tradition of his people, he brings Mary back to his home for the wedding ceremony. She is as happy as a queen. All the way to Joseph's house, the wedding party celebrates. Friends and family play music and sing songs with joyful hearts. When the party arrives at the groom's house, a long prayer shawl is placed over the heads of the future husband and wife. This is a sign that Joseph and Mary agree always to live together under one roof. Then they promise to love and be faithful to each other.

"I, Joseph, son of Jacob, promise before God and before all those present here that I will always look after you and protect you. Mary, do you want to be my wife?"

"Yes, I do!" Mary exclaims, with a radiant smile.

Let the party continue! After having their fill of good food and drink, the men get up to dance. They lift Mary up and carry her along with them in their dance. Just look at the joyful spring in their step as they leap to the rhythm of the music! Never in all of Galilee was there a more beautiful wedding feast. Some even say the festivities will last for several days, because everyone is so happy!

Mary and Joseph travel to Bethlehem

One morning, many months later, while Mary is sweeping the front of her house, she sees Joseph returning from town. He looks upset – I would even say very upset. Mary puts away her broom and goes to meet him.

"You look worried, my darling Joseph. What's wrong?" she asks.

Joseph answers, "Just now, when I was passing by the synagogue, I learned that the Emperor Augustus says everyone must travel to their home town as soon as possible to be counted in the census. He wants to know how many people are in the empire."

The Wonderful Story of Christmas

Cut-outs

INSTRUCTIONS

This section of cut-outs will allow you to take part in creating the wonderful story of Christmas and have fun at the same time. Here you will find posters to decorate your walls and figures for your own Christmas crèche. It's really easy – all you have to do is follow the instructions!

Step 1
Take this section out of the book by removing the staple in the middle (look for the letter A). Be careful not to hurt yourself or tear the paper.

Step 2
Once this section is out, remove the two staples that hold the pages together (look for the letter B). With the pages separated, it will be easier for you to cut.

Step 3
Cut along the dotted lines for posters to put on the wall.

Step 4
Carefully cut out the figures for the crèche.

Step 5
Using coloured paper and cardboard, make your own backgrounds:

- *a stable, where you can place the figures you have cut out*
- *a manger for the animals, using paper straw, where you can place the infant Jesus*
- *other things, such as trees, flowers, stars, the moon, animals and other characters you'd like to add.*

Your crèche, which you and I created together, will be unique. Have your scissors, glue and paper ready, and you can get to work!

Jesus

Mary

Joseph

The shepherds

Balthasar

Melchior

Caspar

"We must go, then," Mary replies. "Joseph, look at me! I believe you don't want to go to your home town. Am I mistaken?"

"It's not that I don't want to go, it's just…"

"It's just what?"

"It's just that you're about to have a baby and Bethlehem is a long way from here. That's what's bothering me," Joseph says. He sounds a little impatient.

"Don't worry about that, Joseph," Mary answers. "We have enough time before the baby comes to make the trip not just once, but even twice. Go and find a donkey. We had better hurry. We'll need to leave soon if we want to get a room at one of the inns there."

They pack some food and clothing and are on their way.

The inns are all full

Mary and Joseph finally arrive in Bethlehem. They are tired from their long journey.

"What a big crowd of people!" Joseph says, looking around.

"I'm sorry, what did you say? Were you talking to me, Joseph?"

"Yes. What is it, Mary? Is something wrong?"

"I think the baby is going to come soon!"

"What? But you told me there was lots of time!"

"I was wrong. Please, let's find a room so I can rest a little."

"You stay right here," he says tenderly. "I'm going to see that innkeeper over there. Maybe he will have room for us."

"Good evening, sir," Joseph says to the innkeeper. "Do you have a room for us? My wife is about to give birth and we have nowhere to stay."

"Don't you know that there is a census and all the inns are full?" answers the innkeeper. He would rather finish cooking his dinner than look after this stranger.

"I beg you, all we need is a sheltered spot with a little warmth…"

"Well, there's the stable in the field behind the inn," the innkeeper says. "My ox sleeps there when the nights are cool."

"Since you have nothing else, your ox and my donkey can keep the baby and its mother warm. Thank you, sir." Joseph runs back to Mary, shouting, "I found us a place!"

"You found a room?" she says happily.

"Well, no, not quite. It's more like a stable than a room."

"Like a stable?" she says in astonishment.

"Yes, but I think it'll be fine. Let's go. It's not far. You can rest there."

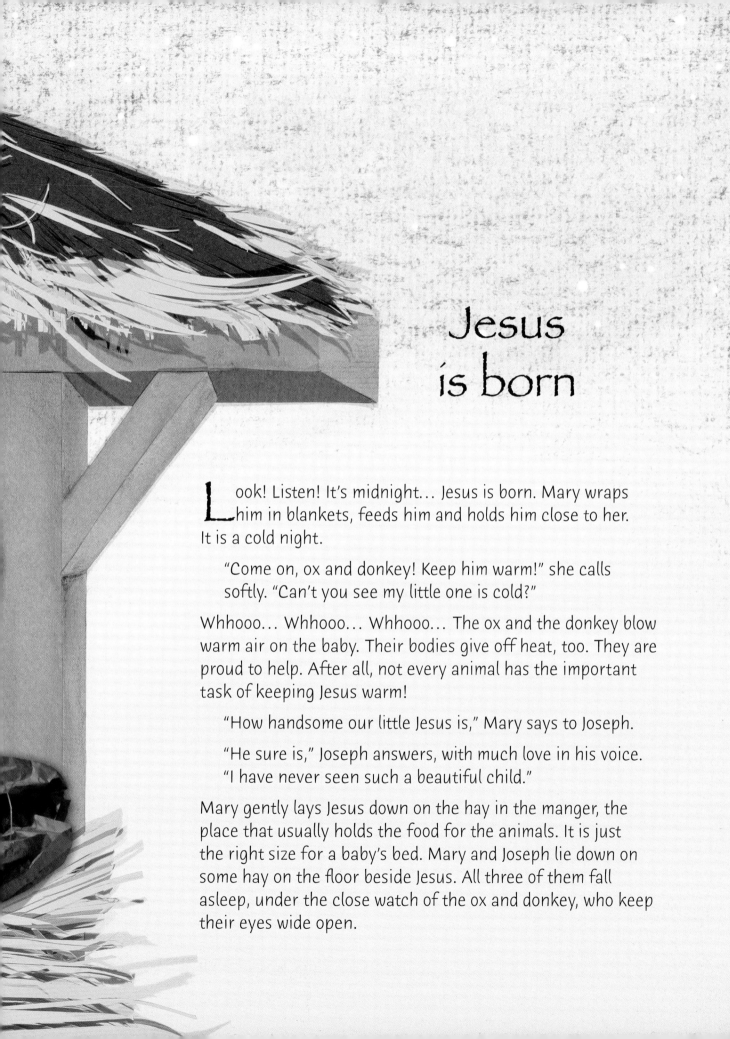

Jesus is born

Look! Listen! It's midnight… Jesus is born. Mary wraps him in blankets, feeds him and holds him close to her. It is a cold night.

"Come on, ox and donkey! Keep him warm!" she calls softly. "Can't you see my little one is cold?"

Whhooo… Whhooo… Whhooo… The ox and the donkey blow warm air on the baby. Their bodies give off heat, too. They are proud to help. After all, not every animal has the important task of keeping Jesus warm!

"How handsome our little Jesus is," Mary says to Joseph.

"He sure is," Joseph answers, with much love in his voice. "I have never seen such a beautiful child."

Mary gently lays Jesus down on the hay in the manger, the place that usually holds the food for the animals. It is just the right size for a baby's bed. Mary and Joseph lie down on some hay on the floor beside Jesus. All three of them fall asleep, under the close watch of the ox and donkey, who keep their eyes wide open.

The shepherds visit

As soon as Jesus is born, choirs of angels fill the countryside to announce the good news far and wide. They sing so loud that they wake up all the sheep and shepherds in the area.

"A Child of light is born to you, a Saviour," they sing. "You will find him in the stable, wrapped in blankets and asleep on the hay. Go, shepherds! He is waiting for you. He wants you to be the first to come to the manger."

The shepherds all set out, singing as they go. They go to search for this holy child.

When they arrive at the stable, they find the whole family asleep. Without making any noise, each one slowly moves up to get a closer look at the baby. They gaze at him with love.

"Baaaa," bleats one of the sheep, as if it wanted to wake Jesus up to greet him. The sheep is quickly taken out of the stable, but…too late, the holy family is awake now. Jesus starts to cry.

The shepherds feel bad about this. They want to leave right away.

"No, don't go," Mary begs them. "It's a good thing you woke us. My poor little fellow must be hungry." Mary feeds Jesus and he is calm again.

The shepherds are filled with wonder. They offer Jesus their most beautiful lambs as gifts. As they leave, they promise to spread the good news about Jesus' birth to everyone they meet.

The wise men come

Around the same time, three astronomers in three different faraway countries see something very special in the night sky. These astronomers look at the sky every night to study the stars. Tonight, a star that is much brighter than any other has appeared in the sky. This star feels like an invitation to everyone in the world. The astronomers know it means someone important has been born.

How do they know? Who told them? No one knows. Nor do we know much about them. Only that there are three of them, they are called the wise men and they come

from very far away. They follow the star for many days. The Bible doesn't tell us their names, but stories that have been handed down since that time do.

First there is Balthasar, who legend tells us has made his journey from Africa on the back of a lion. He presents Jesus with a gift of frankincense. Following close behind is Caspar, who is from a western country. He has travelled on horseback. He has brought Jesus a gift of myrrh. Finally, there is Melchior, who has arrived by camel from Asia. He offers Jesus a gift of gold. Three gifts worthy of the greatest of kings!

And that is the wonderful story of Christmas.

Many people have made crèches, or nativity scenes, but the first one was made by St. Francis of Assisi, in Italy.

Nearly 800 years ago, in 1223, this kind monk wanted to do something special on Christmas night, the night Jesus was born. He asked his friends to bring a few animals to a grotto – a kind of cave – in the middle of the forest where a priest was going to celebrate midnight mass with the people. There was an ox, a donkey and some sheep. The story tells us that a beautiful baby was sleeping in a manger there, just as Jesus had done long, long ago. The animals kept the baby warm with their breath. I'm sure St. Francis would have given the baby a big hug that night.

Maybe you, like St. Francis, will get the idea of telling the wonderful story of Christmas to your family or friends in your own way.

Merry Christmas to all!

Claude Lafortune

© 2003 Novalis, Saint Paul University, Ottawa, Canada

Conception and creation:
Claude Lafortune

Assistance with the construction of the characters:
Pierre Régimbald

Photography:
Claude Lacasse

Graphic design:
Mardigrafe inc.

Business Office:
Novalis
49 Front Street East, 2nd Floor
Toronto, Ontario, Canada
M5E 1B3

Phone: 1-800-387-7164 or (416) 363-3303
Fax: 1-800-204-4140 or (416) 363-9409
E-mail: cservice@novalis.ca
www.novalis.ca

ISBN: 2-89507-438-0   C2003-903461-5 (perfect-bound)
ISBN: 2-89507-439-9   C2003-903460-7 (saddle-stitched)

We acknowledge the financial support of the Government of Canada through the Book Publishing Industry Development Program (BPIDP) for our publishing activities.

5 4 3 2 1   07 06 05 04 03

The author would like to thank the team that produced the play The Wonderful Story of Christmas – Paul Buissonneau, Pierre Régimbald, Gabriel Brochu, Raynald Michaud, Mario Bouchard, Martine Rozon, Éric Belley, Viviane Rheault and Christine Huart – as well as the staff of the Just for Laughs Museum in Montreal for their friendly collaboration.